# FORTNITE BATTLE ROYALE HACKS: MOBILE

# FORTNITE BATTLE ROYALE HACKS:
## MOBILE

### AN UNOFFICIAL GUIDE TO TIPS AND TRICKS THAT OTHER GUIDES WON'T TEACH YOU

## JASON R. RICH

Sky Pony Press
New York

Copyright © 2018 by Hollan Publishing, Inc.

Fortnite® is a registered trademark of Epic Games, Inc.

The Fortnite game is copyright © Epic Games, Inc.

Sky Pony Press books may be purchased in bulk at special discounts for sales promotion, corporate gifts, fund-raising, or educational purposes. Special editions can also be created to specifications. For details, contact the Special Sales Department, Sky Pony Press, 307 West 36th Street, 11th Floor, New York, NY 10018 or info@ skyhorsepublishing.com.

Sky Pony® is a registered trademark of Skyhorse Publishing, Inc.®, a Delaware corporation.

Visit our website at www.skyponypress.com.

Authors, books, and more at SkyPonyPressBlog.com.

10 9 8 7 6 5 4 3 2 1

Library of Congress Cataloging-in-Publication Data is available on file.

Cover design by Brian Peterson

Print ISBN: 978-1-5107-4336-6
Ebook ISBN: 978-1-5107-4337-3

Printed in the United States of America

# TABLE OF CONTENTS

# SECTION 1

## EXPERIENCE *FORTNITE: BATTLE ROYALE* WHILE ON-THE-GO

If you've already experienced the action and intensity of *Fortnite: Batt* *Royale* on your PC, Mac, Xbox One, PS4, or Nintendo Switch gamin *stem*, you already know just how fun and challenging participating lo, Duo, or Squad matches can be.

Thanks to the iOS mobile edition of *Fortnite: Battle Royale*, if you're pple iPhone and iPad user, you can now experience the same rea me action and combat virtually anywhere, as long as your mob

pic Games has announced it'll release an Android-based version
ortnite: Battle Royale in Summer 2018, allowing an even larger grou
smartphone and tablet users to experience the mysteries and cor
at that unfold on the infamous island.

## Get Ready to Tap Your Survival and Combat Skills

hen you experience *Fortnite: Battle Royale*, you take on the role
brave soldier who gets transported, via the flying Battle Bus, to
mote island.

bing from the flying bus and freefalling toward the gro
g your glider to achieve a safe landing, you'll soon find
and—armed only with a pickaxe.

ame time you arrive on the island, up to 99 othe
ed in real time by other gamers) are also transp
d. From this moment forward, everyone has just of
—survival!

To make surviving on the island a bit more challenging, just minutes after each match kicks off, a deadly storm materializes and begins to make portions of the island uninhabitable. Shown here, the soldier is stuck inside the storm and running to escape it before his health points and shields are depleted by the damage caused by the storm.

To stay safe, you'll need to avoid the storm as it slowly expands and moves. Areas of the island map displayed in pink have already been devastated by the storm. Ideally, you'll want to avoid these areas. As a match progresses, the amount of damage you'll receive for each second you stay in the storm increases.

ltimately, the storm forces all remaining soldiers into the final c
e—a very tiny (but random) area of the island, where the End Gam
kes place. With only two soldiers remaining in the match that's show
ere, one player is rushing the other player's fortress by building a ram
o reach a higher level than his opponent. Notice the map displayed
he top-left corner of the screen shows that almost the entire islan
xcept for the final circle, has been ravaged by the storm.

uring each match, one soldier must defeat all others to survive. W
ou be that soldier? At the end of a match, only one soldier will achiev
hat's known as *#1 Victory Royale*. Everyone else will perish! There
o second place.

## You Have Several Responsibilities During Each Match

Each *Fortnite: Battle Royale* match lasts approximately 15 minutes. Throughout a match, your soldier has nine primary responsibilities:

1. Focus on survival
2. Avoid the deadly storm
3. Safely explore the island
4. Gather resources (wood, stone, and metal)
5. Build structures, ramps, and fortresses as they're needed
6. Find, collect, and use a wide range of weapons and ammunition
7. Acquire and use various loot items that can help you stay alive
8. Engage in combat against enemy soldiers
9. Prepare for the End Game (also referred to as the Final Circle).

To become the last soldier standing, you'll need to outsmart and out-fight all of your enemies. You'll need to find and choose the best weapons, ammo, and loot items to carry with you and use, based on the many different types of combat situations you'll encounter, the type of terrain you're currently in, and the strategies your enemies are using in their attempt to defeat you. You'll need to make many split-second decisions, and then take action or react faster than your opponents.

This unofficial strategy guide teaches you many strategies that'll help you stay alive longer, defeat more enemies, and handle yourself like a pro in a wide range of combat situations throughout each match. However, knowing what you need to do (and when to do it) is only part of the challenge. It'll take a lot of practice before you're able to survive entire matches and make it into the End Game.

## How to Download and Install *Fortnite: Battle Royale* onto Your Mobile Device

One reason why *Fortnite: Battle Royale* has become so popular is because it's free to play! All you need to do is download and install the *Fortnite* app onto your smartphone or tablet, and then set up a free Epic Games account. However, if you already have an Epic Games account and play *Fortnite: Battle Royale* on a computer- or console-based gaming system, use the same account information when you play on your mobile device.

To download and install *Fortnite* onto your iPhone or iPad, follow these steps:

1. From the **Home** screen of your iPhone or iPad, launch the **App Store**. Your iPhone or iPad must be running iOS 11 (or iOS 12) and be connected to the Internet.
2. Tap on the **Search** icon displayed at the bottom of the screen.
3. Within the **Search field**, type: *Fortnite*, and then press the **Search key** on the virtual keyboard.
4. Tap on the **Get** button associated with the **Fortnite** app.
5. When prompted, enter your **Apple ID password**, or use the Touch ID or Face ID feature of your iPhone or iPad to confirm your request.
6. Once the app is downloaded and installed, tap on the **Open** button to launch the game, or from the **Home** screen, tap on the **Fortnite** app icon.

One of the first things you'll need to do is set up a free Epic Games account. You can do this from within the app, or by visiting: **https:// accounts.epicgames.com/register**. If you already have an Epic Games account, be sure to sign into the game using that account information.

Each time Epic Games updates the *Fortnite: Battle Royale* game, your mobile device will need to download and install the free update. This will require downloading almost 1GB of data. If you have a 4G/LTE cellular data plan with a monthly wireless data allocation, you should seriously consider using a Wi-Fi Internet connection instead so you don't quickly use up your available data by updating the game.

Ultimately, when you begin playing *Fortnite: Battle Royale* on your smartphone or tablet, you can use either a cellular data or Wi-Fi internet connection, but since you'll use up a lot of data playing, a Wi-Fi connection typically makes the most sense.

If you're using an Android-based smartphone or tablet, acquire the *Fortnite: Battle Royale* app from the Google Play Store, using the same steps you'd follow to find and download any optional app. For more information, visit **www.fortnite.com** and click on the Download button that's displayed near the top-right corner of the browser window.

## The Cost of Playing *Fortnite: Battle Royale*

Not only is the *Fortnite: Battle Royale* mobile app free, but it's also free to actually play the game! However, optional in-app purchases are available. From within the app, you can purchase V-Bucks (game currency) using real money. V-Bucks are then used to acquire specific things within the game itself.

The Lobby is shown here on an iPhone. As you can see, the information displayed on the screen looks virtually identical to what's seen on the iPad.

From the *Fortnite: Battle Royale* Lobby (shown here on the iPad), visit the Store to purchase V-Bucks. The Store icon is displayed near the top-center of the Lobby screen.

Once you access the Store, you can buy 1,000 V-Bucks for $9.99, 2,800 V-Bucks for $24.99, 7,500 V-Bucks for $59.99, or 13,500 V-Bucks for $99.99. By purchasing larger bundles of V-Bucks, you can later save money when making other in-app purchases.

## What Can Be Purchased Using V-Bucks

Here's a summary of what you can purchase within the *Fortnite: Battle Royale* game using V-Bucks.

## Battle Passes

Every three months or so, a new Season of *Fortnite: Battle Royale* kicks off. In conjunction with each new Season, Epic Games introduces major game enhancements, adds new points of interest to the map, makes new weapons and loot items available, and introduces new storylines. A new Battle Pass also begins.

A Battle Pass is a series of daily, weekly, and Tier-based challenges that players can optionally complete in order to unlock rare and limited-edition items. These items are used to customize your character. When you purchase a Battle Pass, you'll be invited to complete all of the new challenges offered during the current Season, in order to unlock special items. At the end of each Season, the current Battle Pass ends and a new one can be purchased.

To acquire a Battle Pass, first go to the Store (from the Lobby screen) and purchase V-Bucks. Next, from the Lobby, tap on the Battle Pass option (located near the top-center of the screen) to acquire the current Battle Pass.

If you don't purchase a Battle Pass, you can still complete certain challenges for free, but the items you're able to unlock will be less exciting than the rare and limited-edition items you'll unlock if you've acquired a Battle Pass.

## lock Battle Pass Tiers

e you purchase a Battle Pass, if you don't want to complete e he challenges within each Tier of the Battle Pass, you can opt purchase the ability to unlock one Battle Pass Tier at a time. is 150 V-Bucks per Tier. By paying to unlock a Tier, you'll insta ire the items offered within that Tier. As items are unlocked, laced within your Locker.

## m Shop Items

nin the Item Shop, Epic Games offers a new selection of opti s that can be purchased, one at a time.

n day, the Item Shop displays three Featured Items, which typi des at least one or two rare or limited-edition outfits, as we optional Pickaxe, Glider, and/or Back Bling design that matches ured outfit(s). These items are sold separately. At least four [

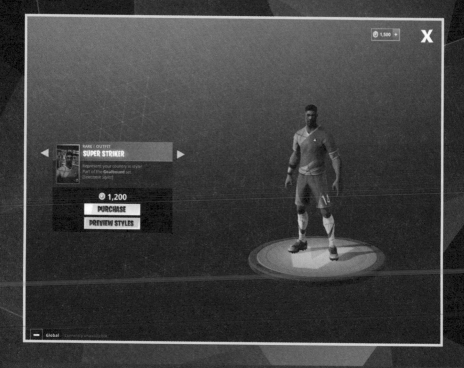

Each limited-edition or rare outfit typically costs between 1,000 and 2,000 V-Bucks. The Super Striker outfit that's shown here costs 1,200 V-Bucks. If you want the matching Glider and Pickaxe design for this outfit, each will cost an additional 500 V-Bucks.

Keep in mind, anything you purchase from the Item Shop (or acquire by completing challenges) can be used to customize the appearance of your soldier. These items do not enhance the strength, speed, agility, or fighting capabilities of the character. They're for cosmetic purposes only. However, most gamers love to customize the appearance of their soldier.

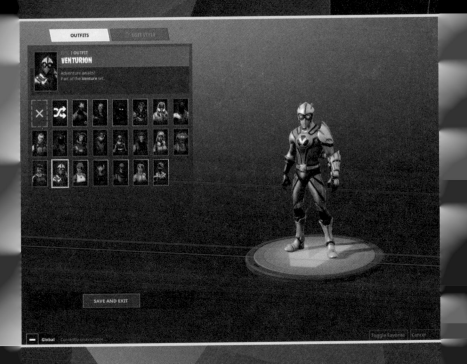

ll items you acquire or unlock get stored within your Locker. Show ere is the selection of outfits within the Locker that have been prev usly purchased or acquired. You can visit the Locker before each matc change the appearance of your soldier, plus determine which emot u'll have access to during the game. Only items you've previously pu hased, unlocked, or acquired will be available to you from the Locke

## *Fortnite: Battle Royale* Is Continuously Evolving

ne of the great things about playing *Fortnite: Battle Royale* is th very week or two, Epic Games issues a new game update that ofte cludes new weapons, loot items, map locations, and other tweaks he game. In addition, new (but temporary) gameplay modes are som mes introduced—all of which provide new and exciting challenges.

At the start of Season 5 (in July 2018), for example, Epic Games added this this Viking village and ship at the top of a mountain (near map coordinates B5.5). While it's not labeled on the map, like all newly added locations, it quickly become a popular landing destination.

This strategy guide was compiled near the beginning of *Fortnite: Battle Royale* Season 5. As a result, it covers the map locations (points of interest), loot items, and gameplay elements that currently existed within the game. When you begin playing, however, there will likely be new additions within the game, and other gameplay elements may have been removed or tweaked.

To discover what's new, be sure to visit the Epic Games website at: www.epicgames.com/fortnite/en-US/news.

To ensure you're able to see the most detail possible within this guide, almost all screenshots from *Fortnite: Battle Royale* were taken using an iPad Pro. Regardless of what smartphone or tablet you're using, the screens should look almost identical.

# SECTION 2
## CUSTOMIZE YOUR GAMEPLAY EXPERIENCE

If you're a *Fortnite* noob (beginner), chances are all of the default settings for the HUD (heads up display) and options available from the Settings menus will work just fine. As you get more acquainted with the game, however, you might choose to tweak some of the options, so that they work better with your personal gameplay style.

During a match, you'll often switch between **Combat** mode and **Building** mode. When in Combat mode, your soldier can use any weapon within his backpack to fight. You'll switch to Building mode to build a ramp, structure, or fortress, for example.

When in Combat mode you cannot build.

When in Building mode (shown here), you can't fight using any weapons (including the pickaxe). Thus, it's essential that you practice quickly switching between these two modes as it becomes necessary during each match.

## How to Adjust the Customizable HUD

The HUD Layout Tool allows you to adjust the size and location of the on-screen controls that are displayed throughout each match.

From the Lobby, tap on the **Menu** icon that's displayed in the top-right corner of the screen. It looks like three horizontal lines.

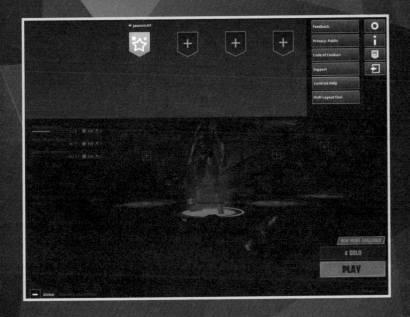

Tap on the **Controls Help** button to see the default layout for your on-screen controls when in Combat and Build mode.

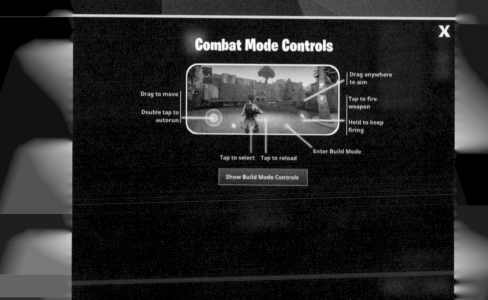

is the default Combat Mode Controls layout.

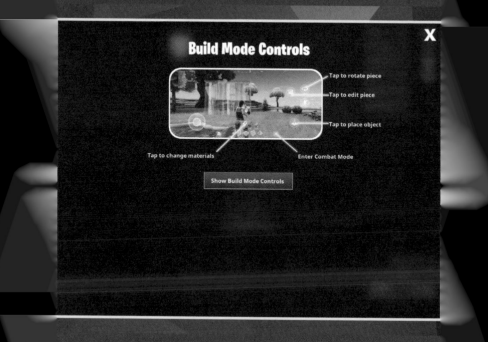

is the default Build Mode Controls layout.

# CUSTOMIZE YOUR GAMEPLAY EXPERIENCE

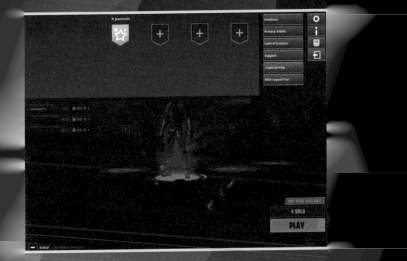

ize and edit the default Combat Mode Controls
trols layouts, from the Lobby, after tapping on
n the **HUD Layout Tool** button.

t **Combat** mode looks like during a match. Notice t
on. Memorize this information, so you can tap ic
ut paying too much attention. The common actio
n Combat mode include: walking, running, jumpir
ing, choosing a weapon, aiming a weapon, and
ou're also able to check your Backpack Inventory

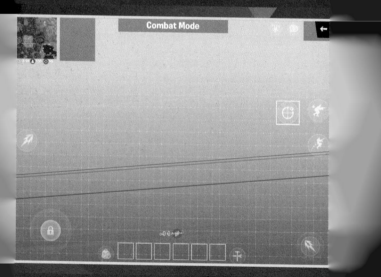

access the HUD Layout Tool, first choose Com
le to reposition and often resize each of the icons o
ace your finger on one icon at a time to move it are
desired location on the screen. Make sure that w
our smartphone or tablet, you're able to easily reac
fingers when playing.

an icon, tap on it to select it. A box will appear a
e, the Aim icon is selected. Next, tap on the black
ing arrow icon that's displayed in the top-right co

Size scroll bar to the left to shrink the size of the
the scroll bar to the right to increase the size of th
the same with the Display Scale slider, if you ch
ows you to adjust the size of the selected icon, cor
t size of the other icons. Tap the Exit button wh
sting the size of each icon.

ur changes, tap on the Confirm button when this Sa

t Build mode looks like during a match. While
e to help your soldier move around, select b
ouilding material, rotate the selected buildin
eces on the island (to build ramps, structures, a
dit structures to add windows and doors, for ex
o check your Backpack Inventory, access the is
Combat mode.

ing a structure or fortress, for example, you're
example, you can add windows or a door to fo
build and edit structures is covered in "Sectio
and Building."

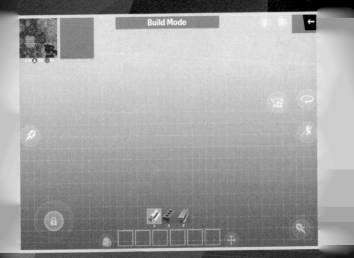

...access the HUD Layout Tool, when Build mode ... to reposition and resize each on-screen icon, on... ...did when customizing the Combat mode controls... ...hanges.

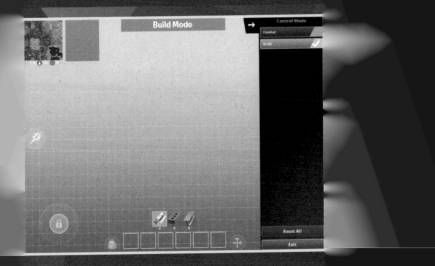

...e size and location of each icon, in both Comba... ...eir default settings, once again access the HUD L... ...e black-and-white, left-pointing arrow icon, and... ...de menu (shown here on the right side of the s... ...et All button. When the Reset All Settings non-

## How to Adjust the Settings Menu Options

Just like the PC, Mac, and console versions of *Fortnite: Battle Royale*, the mobile version allows you to customize a handful of gameplay and sound-related settings. If you desire, this can be done before each match. However, once you adjust any of the Settings options and save your changes, those changes remain active until you again change them or reset them manually.

To access the Settings menu from the Lobby, tap on the Menu icon that's displayed in the top-right corner of the screen. (It looks like three horizontal bars.)

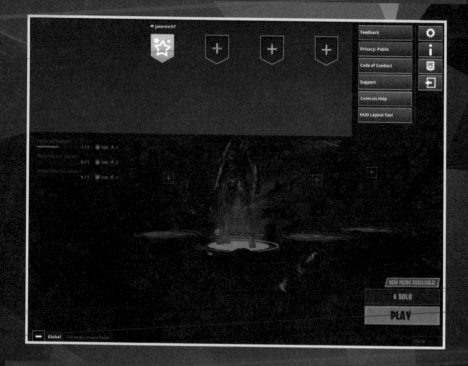

From the menu displayed in the top-right corner of the screen, tap on the gear-shaped Game Settings icon. As you can see, it too is located in the very top-right corner of the screen.

**CUSTOMIZE YOUR GAMEPLAY EXPERIENCE**

| Game | | | |
|---|---|---|---|
| **Region** | | | |
| Language | ◀ English ▶ | ⓘ |
| Matchmaking Region | ◀ Auto (25ms) ▶ | ⓘ |
| **Input** | | | |
| Touch Sensitivity | 0.47 | ⓘ |
| Touch ADS Sensitivity | 0.67 | ⓘ |
| Touch Scope Sensitivity | 0.67 | ⓘ |
| Vertical Sensitivity Multiplier | 1.00 | ⓘ |
| Invert View | ◀ Off ▶ | ⓘ |
| **Control Options** | | | |
| Sprint Cancels Reloading | ◀ Off ▶ | ⓘ |
| Tap to Search / Interact | ◀ Off ▶ | ⓘ |
| Aim Assist | ◀ On ▶ | ⓘ |
| Edit Mode Aim Assist | ◀ On ▶ | ⓘ |
| Reset Building Choice | ◀ Off ▶ | ⓘ |
| Turbo Building | ◀ On ▶ | ⓘ |
| Auto Material Change | ◀ On ▶ | ⓘ |

n here is the Game Settings menu. At the top-center of the s ree Settings-related icons. On the left is the Game Settings middle is the Game Sound icon. On the right is the Accoun nt icon. Tap on each icon, one at a time, to reveal a se enu.

ng with the Game Settings menu, you'll see a handful of us le options. Some have sliders that allow you to adjust the y" of certain gaming features or controls. Other options o d on or off.

reviewing the Game Settings menu, tinker with each sett eem necessary. How you adjust these options is a matter o taste, based on your skill and gaming style. If you discov t *Fortnite* player's Settings-related options, don't just se o be identical. Make adjustments that work well for you p his will probably require some experimentation and tinker oart.

n the Reset Game To Default button (located near the bottom r of the screen) to return all Game Settings, Game Sound nt and Content menu settings to their defaults

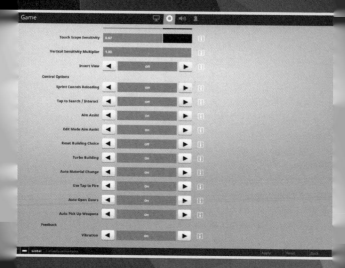

o scroll down when viewing the Game Settings men
ole options.

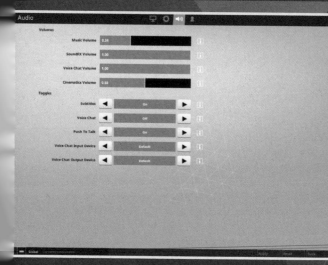

Game Sound menu (shown here), adjust sound-rela
e game. It's essential that you hear the in-game sou
a good strategy to boost the Sound FX Volume opt
r the Music Volume level to a setting that's comf
u're be playing with teammates in Duos or Squads
turning on and customizing other sound-related c
t Volume, and Push to Talk, is important.

## tely Use Headsets When Playing!

laying *Fortnite: Battle Royale* on any mobile device, d
eadset (or earbuds) so you hear all of the sound effects
martphone or tablet has a headphone jack, use a head
n jack. Otherwise, invest in Bluetooth (wireless) heac
ids that also have a microphone built in (which is usef
the team-oriented gameplay modes). Headphones wi
ng technology work extra well, so you can block out all
id avoid distractions.

rely on the speakers built into your mobile device, b
uble hearing the subtle sound effects that are importar
e, like the sound of footsteps or weapon fire.

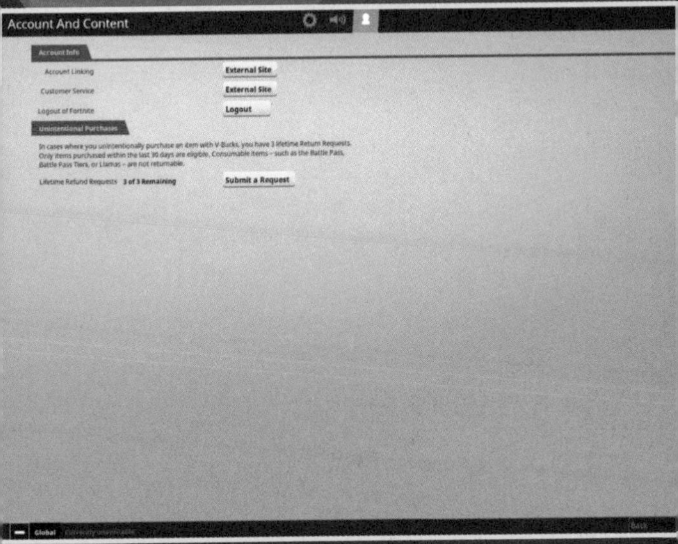

e Account and Content menu (shown here), you ca
elated to your Epic Games account, plus obtain a refunc
purchases you made by mistake. (This refund option
three times.)

ut of the Settings menu, tap on the Back button that's d
iwer-right corner of the screen. You'll be returned to th

One feature that makes aiming and shooting at enemies easier (especially if you're a noob) is the Auto Fire option. When you point a weapon at an enemy, the game will fire your weapon automatically for you. You can also choose the Tap Anywhere or Dedicated Button option, so you can control when you fire your soldier's weapon.

# SECTION 3

## HOW TO CUSTOMIZE YOUR CHARACTER'S APPEARANCE

One of the coolest things about *Fortnite: Battle Royale* is your ability to customize the appearance of your soldier in a variety of ways. Some of these customization items can be unlocked while playing. Others are available for free through promotional partners, like Twitch. tv and Amazon Prime.

If you're a paid Amazon Prime subscriber and have a free Twitch.tv subscription, free *Fortnite* item collections are periodically offered. Visit **https://twitch.amazon.com/prime** for more information.

### Examples of Previously Released Soldier Outfits

Check out these six examples out of the hundreds of limited edition and rare outfits already released by Epic Games.

This optional outfit is called

Raven was a popular outfit that

The Wukong outfit was considered "legendary," and is very rare.

Some outfits, like Tomatohead, look comical.

Cuddle Team Leader is another rare, "legendary," and more whimsical outfit that was released for a limited time.

As part of the Neon Glow set, this Nitelite outfit was released.

Every day new, limited edition or rare character customization items are offered by Epic Games. These must be purchased. From the Lobby, first go to the Store and purchase V-Bucks using real money. Then, use those V-Bucks to purchase one optional item a

## Discover Multiple Ways to Customize Your Soldier

y purchasing, acquiring, and unlocking items, you can customize yo
ldier in a variety of ways.

## Outfits

ach outfit is sold separately and costs between 500 and 2,000 V-buc
hich translates roughly to between $5.00 and $20.00 each). From th
m Shop, tap on one of the outfits displayed to purchase it.

fter selecting an outfit, you'll be prompted to confirm your purchas
ecision, assuming you have enough V-Bucks in your account. Tap c
e Purchase button to buy the outfit (in this case, for 1,200 V-Bucks
his Aerial Threat soccer-themed outfit can be customized by count
ter it's purchased. Tap on the Preview Styles option prior to purcha
g it.

...ng on the Preview Styles button, tap on a coun...
...e of the screen and see its unique uniform desig...
...side of the screen. Here, the United States flag a...
...This outfit was released for a limited time in...
...18 World Cup.

...esign

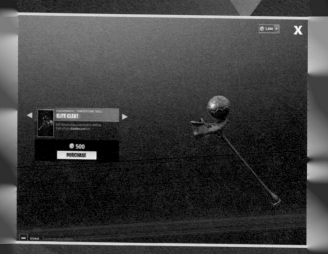

...on with each new outfit, Epic Games releases...
...ese items are sold separately from the Item Sh...
...optional. They typically cost between 500 and 8...

...cquired several pickaxe designs (they're s... ...ols"), from the Locker (shown here), comb... ...t you already own. The pickaxe is an item... ...throughout every match, so it's seen ofte...

...r soldier leaps from the Battle Bus at the s... ...ward the ground. At any time during this... ...the glider (shown here). The glider slows... ...escent and gives you precise navigational... ...location. While all glider designs look di... ...ly the same way. The glider is only seen a... ...n using a Launch Pad during a match.

## ᴈ Design

every match, your soldier wears a backpack. In cc
ew outfit designs, a matching backpack design (r
ng") is sold separately. Plan on spending an addi
cks for each.

each match you're often looking at the back of
ck bling is seen most of the time. Remember, you
tch different outfits with various glider, pickaxe,
s to make your soldier look truly unique.

s

e are three different types of emotes available that can be us
re-deployment area prior to a match, as well as during a matc
r for your soldier to make a statement. These include dance mc
paint tags, and graphic icons.

emotes that are sold by the Item Shop typically cost 500 to
cks each. Others are offered as prizes for completing daily, we
attle Pass Tier-related challenges.

ct a **Dance Move** and your soldier will bust out some awesome
raphy. Since many different dance moves are offered separa
ure to try combining a few moves. Some players use dance m
oat after a victory, or to taunt an opponent during a match.

y **Paint Tags**—Once you've acquired and selected one or mo
e emotes, you can spray paint specific designs on any flat sur

**Graphic Icons**—After unlocking one or more of these icons, your soldier can toss one of them at a time into the air. It'll be displayed for several seconds for everyone around to see.

## Select Customization Items from the Locker

Once you've acquired one or more outfits, back bling designs, glider designs, pickaxe designs, and/or emotes, customize your soldier's appearance from the Locker. You're also able to create and display a custom banner (for free), choose between different contrails you've unlocked, plus choose the loading screen graphic you'll see when the game is first loading.

designs typically need to be unlocked or acquired, as
hased. This is the animated graphic you'll see trailing
ldier during their freefall from the Battle Bus, and so
eir glider has been activated.

of the optional customizations available, the contrail you
pearance purposes only and has no impact on actual ga

om the Locker, follow these steps to customize your character usi
ems currently available to you:

1. Tap on the slot within the Locker for the outfit, for example.
2. From the Outfits menu, choose the one you want your soldie
   to wear.
3. Tap on the Save and Exit button to return to the Locker.

epeat these three steps to choose a custom banner icon, back bli
esign, pickaxe design, glider design, contrail design, and loading scre
esign.

## How to Customize Your Emotes Menu

ter purchasing, acquiring, or unlocking a new emote, it'll becon
vailable to you from the Locker before any match. Tap on the Lock
on, and from the Locker screen (shown here), tap on one of the s
mote boxes displayed below the Emotes heading (on the left side
e screen).

...ote screen displays all of the emotes currently availab... ...time, choose up to six that you'd like available to yo... ...Each time you tap on an emote icon on the left side of t... ...e previewed on the right side of the screen. Here, a da... ...previewed. Tap the Save and Exit button to continue...

...the pre-deployment area or during an actual match,... ...icon that's displayed near the top-right corner of the... ...his Emotes menu. Tap on one of the emotes to use it

When using spray paint tags, you can use several different designs in the same area to leave a personalized mark on your surroundings.

# SECTION 4

## WELCOME TO THE ISLAND! HOW LONG WILL YOU SURVIVE?

Every match you'll experience in *Fortnite: Battle Royale* takes place on the island. This is no ordinary island, however—it's chock full of interesting places to explore, each of which offers a unique setting where intense battles will unfold.

### The Island Map Displays Lots of Useful Information

Checking the island map during a match reveals a lot of useful information, including:

- The random route the Battle Bus will take across the island as it drops you off. This route is only displayed while you're in the pre-deployment area and for the first few seconds while aboard the Battle Bus.
- The location of each point of interest on the island.
- Your current location.
- The location of your teammate(s) if you're experiencing the Duos or Squads gameplay modes, for example.
- The current location of the storm.
- Where the storm will be expanding and moving to next.

When you look at the full screen island map, you'll discover it's divided into quadrants. Along the top of the map are the letters "A" through "J." Along the left edge of the map are the numbers "1" through "10." Each point of interest or location on the map can be found by its unique coordinates.

For example, Lazy Links is located at map coordinates F2.5. Tilted Towers can be found at map coordinates D5.5, and Snobby Shores is located at coordinates A5.

Paradise Palms, one of the newer and more popular areas of the island can be found at map coordinates I8. This area of the island now offers desert terrain, and is one of the places you're most apt to discover a Rift.

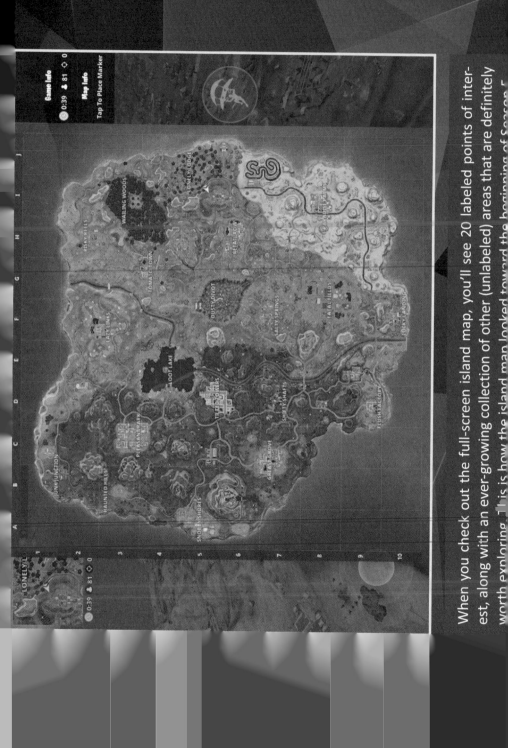

When you check out the full-screen island map, you'll see 20 labeled points of interest, along with an ever-growing collection of other (unlabeled) areas that are definitely worth exploring. This is how the island map looked toward the beginning of Season 5

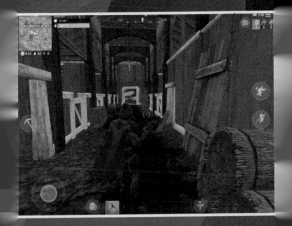

n, displayed in the top-left corner of the sc
ntinuously shows your exact location. A
noving, follow the white line displayed w
fastest way out of the storm's deadly pat
all map to view the more detailed, full-scre
do this when your soldier is in a safe locat
me the victim of an enemy's surprise atta

hanging out in the pre-deployment area
le you're aboard the Battle Bus, be sure
the screen (in the top-left corner of the s
d map. The blue line, which is comprised o
the random route the Battle Bus will tak

e random route the Battle Bus will follow be
us can help you choose your landing locat
irectional controls to navigate while freefalling
ontrol the glider's descent.

o the freefall and aim toward your desired lan
soldier in a downward direction. During free
il approximately halfway across the island be
he route the Battle Bus takes doesn't fly direc
ding location, chances are you'll still be able
you focus on navigation during your descent.

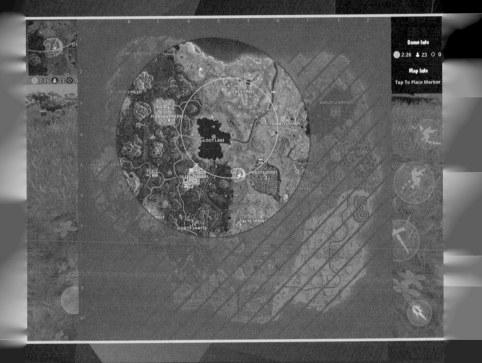

s each match progresses, check the large island map to see what are the island have already been engulfed by the storm. These areas a splayed in pink. The outer circle shows the current safe area.

'hen applicable, the inner circle on the island map shows where tl fe area of the island will be once the storm expands and moves agai e timer that's displayed below the small map indicates when this w ippen. You'll also see warnings about the storm displayed in the ce r of the screen. Plus, right before the storm is about to expand ar ove, you'll hear a ticking sound, followed by a unique storm warnir und effect.

## Explore the Island's Labeled Points of Interest

ne following is information about each of the island's labeled poin ' interest, as well as details about some of the more interesting ar xciting areas of the island that are not labeled on the map.

eep in mind, as each new *Fortnite: Battle Royale* Season kicks off, Ep ames introduces several new points of interest that are labeled. You so discover that some locations that you may already be familiar wi ill experience dramatic alterations or may be removed from the ma together.

s part of the weekly or biweekly game updates that Epic Gam leases, new (unlabeled) points of interest are also periodically adde ) when you play *Fortnite: Battle Royale* for yourself, don't be surprise the island map looks a bit different than what you see in this guide.

/hen you land within a popular point of interest, like Tilted Tower ou'll definitely encounter enemy soldiers almost immediately. Upc nding, take cover and quickly find and grab a weapon so you'll be ab fight. Otherwise, you'll often be shot and defeated within seconds

t on having to engage in fights when visiting
interest. Instead of landing directly in one c
ing in the outskirts. Collect weapons, amn
urrounding structures and areas, and then
est on foot when you're better armed and pr

a popular area and immediately encounter
ing them with your pickaxe and launching a
e several direct hits with the pickaxe to de
g around and moving in between pickaxe s
y the opponent's pickaxe attacks. Howeve
a few seconds before you and managed to
away before you get shot. Here, the sold
too slow for the enemy armed with a weape

look at the labeled points of interest you'll defi
ainted with.

s

dinates: F2.5

s a golf course area that replaced Anarchy Acres

traps of this golf course, you'll often find weap
and/or resources icons lying on the ground.

rain Karts (ATKs) can almost always be found in Lazy Links.
d up golf carts offer the fastest way to get around the islan
r soldiers in a squad can travel together, and the back of
erves as a Bounce Pad. With practice, you'll be able to perfo
of awesome stunts while driving an ATK. Keep in mind, the
shoot while he or she is driving, but passengers can shoc
on they're holding.

## ughout the Island, Be on the Constant Lookout for Che:

ghout the island—mainly within buildings, homes, and
ures, as well as inside of trucks, but sometimes out in the o
discover chests. They have a golden glow and make a sound
et close to them. Open chests to collect a random select
ons, ammo, loot items, and resources. To collect a chest's
you must be the first soldier to open it during a match.

chests are always found within the same spot on the map. C
mly appear during each match, so always be on the looko
(and listen carefully for the sound they make).

/hen you're close to a chest, even if you can't see it, you'll hear ound, and a directional graphic (like the one shown directly above th est) will appear in the center of the screen. This graphic shows you hat direction the chest can be found. Keep in mind, it could be abo r below you, or in any direction around you.

## ty Divot

## Coordinates: Between F5.5 and G5.5

usty Divot tends to be a crowded area, so as you open every doc enter/exit a tunnel, be ready to get ambushed by enemies. In co nction with the start of Season 5, Dusty Divot received a makeove if you were already familiar with this location, be ready to discov mething new. The area is still chock full of chests, as well as weapor mmo, loot items, and resource icons to grab.

was created during Season 4. In the middle of what w
er, are now the remains of a destroyed research facil
e exploring this area, because there is still plenty of g
d grab.

still several structures remaining here. You will disc
ts in this area, so keep your eyes pealed, and liste
und that the chests make.

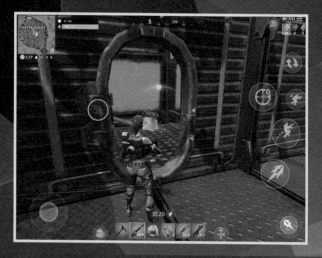

Before Dusty Divot was destroyed, there were tunnels that connected the different structures. Some of these tunnels, as well as the doorways that separated them, still remain. Each time you open a sealed door, you could discover an enemy waiting to ambush you, so be ready to defend yourself. However, within the various rooms that remain, you may find a chest, or something else worth adding to your arsenal.

If you discover other enemy soldiers are in the area, stick to the higher levels, so you'll have a tactical advantage and be able to shoot downward at them. Once the enemy threat is gone, you'll be free to explore this area and reap the benefits of what you collect.

ds

linates: Between F8.5 and G8.5

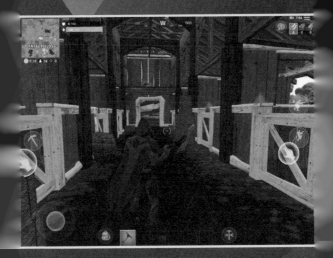

her popular farming area on the island. The lar
ls to explore.

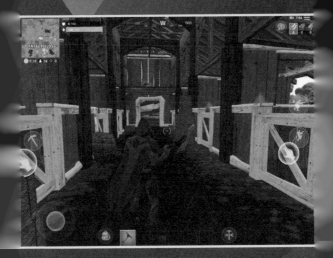

ables, check out each horse stall for useful weap
ems. You'll need to build a ramp to reach the
he loft above the far entrance (which is boarde

...ithin the stable also offer great places to hide. Crou...
...r an enemy soldier to approach, and then ambush...

...r is setting up remote explosives near the boarded...
...le. Once the explosives are set and their blue lights ...
...ble has been booby trapped. This soldier must nov...
...ce, and then wait for an enemy to approach before...
...the explosives.

discover a toilet factory. If you discover enemy soldi
higher levels, and shoot at the soldiers you encour
g below you.

k along the conveyor belts as you explore the fact
er if you stay on the higher levels of the building if t
rs in the vicinity.

short distance from Flush Factory are several buil[...] a dance club. Each of the buildings, including the [...] th weapons, ammo, and loot items, so take time t[...] up your arsenal. Be sure to smash some of the c[...] ucks, and metal items in and around the buildings [...] ash the brick buildings to collect an abundance of s[...]

dance club, search the rooms that surround the d[...] irs) to find chests and other goodies. If you stand in[...] dance floor and another soldier is hiding, you could[...] be out in the open and vulnerable to attack.

**es: Between B7 and C7**

rised of a handful of homes and busin
stores. Inside these buildings, you'll dis
m which you can ambush opponents.

**2.5**

a contains a graveyard and several sma
crypts for weapons, ammo, and loot
and launch a surprise attack if an enem

churches, be sure to explore the tower and basement the stone walls to find hidden chambers and crypt tain chests.

church's tower, use a rifle with a scope to snipe at ene oring below. The tower gives you a great vantage poi u can see almost the entire area.

y high up in this area, which is filled wi
ther junk. You're able to stand on top of
nemies below you. Either that or build a
than everyone else. Don't forget to explor
d this area.

ground level in Junk Junction, you'll ne
e-like area. This is a great place to plan sn
emies. You can also set traps or use remot
ies that pass by.

Located just outside of Junk Junction are several areas that are not labeled on the map. For example, there's the massive soccer stadium, an abandoned motel, and a llama-shaped watchtower. These are all great places to visit if you want to quickly build up your arsenal.

## Lonely Lodge

### Map Coordinates: Between I5 and J5

This is a spread out campground area. Smash the trees to collect wood. Be sure to explore this lodge. Inside there are chests, weapons, ammo, and loot items to be found. Smash the nearby RVs to collect metal.

ice other soldiers exploring this area, hide inside
ns and close the door behind you. As soon as an ene
be ready to blast them with one of your most powe
trategy is to place a trap inside one of the cabins,
e the door as you leave. The next person will be gre
en they enter!

a lot of tiny cabins to search in this area. Howe
and notice a front door is already open, someon
e before you, and they could be hiding inside and
I.

the most exciting places to explore on the island is locat
e Lonely Lodge. It's this giant waterfront mansion.

ou approach the front door of this mansion, instead of er
ur pickaxe to smash the floor. You'll drop into this hidde
in the mansion's basement.

## Loot Lake

### Map Coordinates: E4

Located around this lake are a collection of houses, buildings, and a wooden watchtower. All contain weapons, ammo, and loot items. Some also contain chests. You'll discover this chest near the top of the watchtower.

The two large buildings located along Loot Lake both have several levels and contain chests.

...o directly cross the lake don't walk through i...
...nd leave you vulnerable to attack. Instead, bu...
...oss it, and then move quickly. Be ready to build...
...a shield if you get shot at by someone sniping y...
...you've collected a sniper rifle (or any weapon...
...e hiding spot along the edge of the lake, and...
...rs that attempt to cross the lake.

...iouse that's located near the wooden watch...
...edge of the lake. Explore it just as you wou...
...be on the lookout for items to grab, as well...

too distracted by exploration. Always pay atten... f the storm and the direction it'll be moving next...

## anding

**rdinates: F9.5**

buildings and structures within this region of the... nfluenced design. The large building with a pink t... er often contains a collection of powerful weapon... discover lying on the ground...

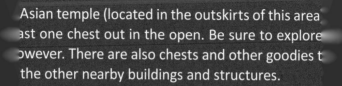

Asian temple (located in the outskirts of this area
ast one chest out in the open. Be sure to explore
owever. There are also chests and other goodies t
the other nearby buildings and structures.

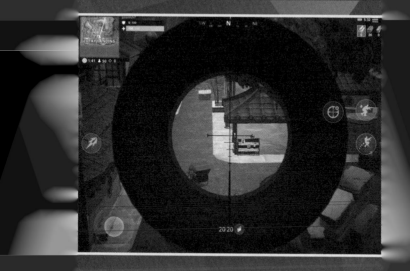

e top of the tallest building in Lucky Landing, an
a rifle (or any gun with a scope) to snipe at enemie
elow. The view from the top level of this building
h of the area from a bird's eye perspective

...hind the counters within the shops and restaur... ...anding. You never know what's waiting to be co... ...the chest's random collection of loot included a...

...e leading in and out of Lucky Landing also has ...esign. You'll find a chest as you cross the bridge, bu... ...the bridge itself and the broken-down vehicles on... ...side of the bridge to the other requires navigating...

Palms

inates: 18

s is a large desert area that replaced Moisty Mi
Near the center of this new region is a small, bu
a bunch of multi-story buildings. Inside the bu
weapons, ammo, and loot.

more fun areas of Paradise Palms is the race t
exploring the buildings that surround the track,
Kart (ATK) and practice your driving skills.

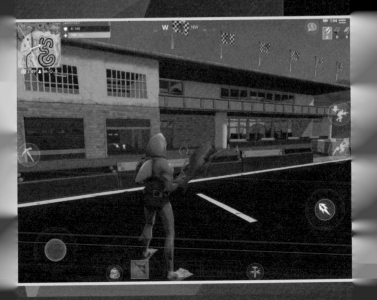

lding surrounding the race track offers some goodies to
n the garage and near the track itself where you're mc
an All Terrain Kart you can hop into and drive.

on to the small city and race track, there are a handful
ork checking out within the island's desert area. For e
small Western town, a truck stop, a lake, and a bunch

rk

ates: **C3.5**

the island contains a bunch of houses, ea
ng. There's also an outdoor soccer field her
r something worth grabbing in the center c
approach it, do so with extreme caution. E
o shoot at you, and you'll be out in the ope
.

of of any home in the area and smash yo
ttic. You're almost always guaranteed to fi
xplore each house, you may discover multip

If you climb to the roof of the structure in the middle of town, and then build a small fortress on top of it, you'll be able to see all around you. Use a mid- or long-range weapon to snipe at enemy soldiers as they move from building to building. On ground level, you'll often find a chest under this structure.

## Retail Row

### Map Coordinates: H6

This too is a popular area of the island. It contains a collection of large stores, restaurants, and businesses, as well as several homes.

op of the water tower (located at the edge of town
you'll typically find a chest or other useful weap
n some metal by smashing the tower.

rs as a shield as you move around outside at grou
m to collect metal. Remember, when you smash car
ise. To make matters worse, the car's alarm will ofte
ate even more noise. This will definitely attract atte
by enemies to your location.

S

nates: H2

movie theater contains a bunch of cars and ash to collect metal. Check within and abov ests or other weapons.

e containing the picnic tables (near the playg s two chests, plus a bunch of weapons and am on the ground. Try to be the first soldier to rea et the best weapons, ammo, and loot items be

Don't forget to search the buildings that surround the theater. Within the concession stand, for example, you'll discover a chest in the bathroom. There will be plenty of useful items out in the open, behind the movie screen, and as you travel between structures in this area.

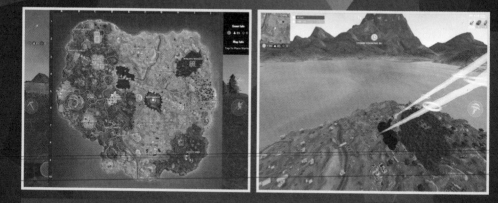

The route the Battle Bus is taking during this trip does not go anywhere near Risky Reels. If this is your intended destination, hop off the bus near Dusty Divot, and soar through the air toward Risky Reels.

By the time the glider activates automatically, you'll be approaching the outskirts of Risky Reels, if you control the direction of your descent.

es: F7

ndful of homes and a gas station, there
he island that's interesting or worth e
visit this area by the moving storm, the
aces on the island to visit. If you do s
s and smash buildings and structures i
(wood, stone, and metal).

es: D7

ng area, you'll discover a collection of
r, the excitement begins when you trav
here are also a few homes nearby that are

The mine tunnels follow a maze-like design, and you can't see around turns. Listen carefully for footsteps, so you don't get surprised and attacked by enemies. It's best to crouch down and tiptoe through this area, so you make the least amount of noise possible.

You'll need to smash through some walls within the mine tunnels to discover this chest. Listen for the sound a chest makes as you explore. You might not see the chest, but you will hear it when you're close. You may also see the glow from the chest emanating through the wooden planks, so pay attention!

**Shores**

**ordinates: A5**

er of mansions in this region of the island are w
eople once lived. Each mansion contains a bunch of
d loot items.

etween the mansions, you can follow the road, smas
alls, or build ramps to climb over the walls that c

st exciting place to visit in this area (at least during S
cret base that's hidden within the nearby mountain. F
it looks like a mountaintop mansion. It can be found
ates B4.5.

ound level in Snobby Shores, build a ramp to reach th
untain. When you see this small structure with a garag
e door open and then travel downward into the mour

the mountain is this secret base. Explore all of the roor
u'll discover several chests, as well as a lot of other w
and loot items scattered around on the ground.

he missile that launched at the end of Season 4, and t
destroyed Moisty Mire. In its place, you'll now find a
own as Paradise Palms. Its within this region of the isla
pt to find Rifts.

## Tilted Towers

### Map Coordinates: D5.5

This is the city region of the island. It contains a bunch of tall buildings, all located close together. This is an extremely popular location, so you're virtually guaranteed to encounter multiple enemy soldiers here. Be ready to fight! Each building contains plenty of weapons, ammo, and loot items to collect. Within many of them, you'll also discover one or more chests. Check out this view from the top of the clock tower. Smash downward to discover multiple chests before you reach ground level. You need to be the first soldier to reach this location, or it's pointless because the chests will already have been emptied. If the top of the clock tower is already gone when you arrive, land elsewhere.

While there are chests and other goodies to be found at ground level, this is one of the most dangerous places to be in Tilted Towers. Be ready to crouch behind vehicles or objects for protection if someone starts shooting at you.

ter off staying as high up as possible and then using
nge weapons (preferably with a scope) to shoot a
m a safe distance. Don't forget, you can shoot or
indows. Enemy soldiers can also enter the building
e.

nage to land before your enemies, grab a weapon a
e clock tower. Shoot at your adversaries as they la

wn

nates: **G4**

traction within this area of the island is a larg...
...t can be found here will be out in the open.

to check behind the counter at the pizza sho...
tables. There's not much to find within the
r gas station. You're better off spending time s...
ses. As always, check the attics, basements, ...
able, for chests.

Tomato Town is one of many locations on the island where you might stumble upon a Vending Machine. If you've gathered enough resources (wood, stone, or metal), you can exchange them for often rare and powerful weapons or loot items. Vending Machines offer a great way to add powerful weapons or loot items used to replenish your health and/or shields to the arsenal you're carrying with you.

If you don't yet have enough resources to purchase the item(s) you want, go out and collect more wood, stone, or metal, and then return to the Vending Machine. Keep in mind, when you're standing in front of a Vending Machine, you're vulnerable to attack. Consider building walls to surround you and the machine. Otherwise, as soon as you make a purchase, a nearby enemy might launch a surprise attack, defeat you, and quickly collect everything you've gathered during the match.

Explore the homes in the area, and don't forget to visit the basement, garage, and/or attic, if applicable.

se forest portion of the island. Smash dov
e you're here. Make your way to the cente
iscover a hedge maze, along with a wat
the maze and tower are chests, as well

ing on ground level and walking through tl
p of the hedge walls and walk on them, s
you a tactical advantage if you need to s
. You could also try landing on top of th
nedge maze, and then smash your way c

mer activated a Port-a-Fort in the middle of the he the top of it, was able to pick off several enemi explored the hedge maze. The Port-a-Fort gave a height advantage from a tactical standpoint, p rotection.

the ground within the woods is what appears o an underground bunker. At the end of Season of Season 5, it was not possible to open or damag e. Its purpose will likely be revealed sometime in

## Discover Some of the Island's Unlabeled Areas

As you travel between labeled points of interest, or if you choose to roam freely around the island, you're sure to encounter many interesting places. Here are a few spots you don't want to miss.

Located at map coordinates B6 is what's now a Viking village. Here you'll discover multiple structures to explore, as well as a large Viking ship. It's easiest to land on the top of this mountain after leaping from the Battle Bus, but there is a trail you can follow from ground level.

Located between map coordinates D2 and E2, you'll discover an abandoned motel. The guestrooms and the structures surrounding the main motel area are worth visiting if you want to expand your arsenal and stock up on ammo. This decrepit motel is just a short distance from Lazy Links. You can land here to build your arsenal before heading toward the gold course, or visit Lazy Links first, hop into an ATK, and then drive to the motel's location.

near the edge of the island, within the desert area
ates I9.5) is a Western village that's loaded with che
oodies. Once you're done exploring here, step into a
t yourself toward your next desired destination. Be
e storm's path.

p coordinates C1, just a short walk from the massive
ou'll discover this movie set area. Be sure to visit th

map coordinates I5.5, you'll discover this RV par
he RVs you'll find some useful things to pick up, but
f can be found in the buildings that surround this
d on top of the RVs and jump from one to the other i
a height advantage in case enemy soldiers are lurk
e RVs to collect a lot of metal.

ap coordinates D8, you'll come across a giant woo
a few buildings and homes that are worth taking

nates E9, you'll encounter a cluster of bu
ned dance club. Take a moment to practi
dance floor but be careful you don't get sni
chests are located in other areas of this buil
be thorough. Don't neglect exploring th
structures as well while you're in the area.

it map coordinates H4.5 to discover this
there's a maze-like area of storage contair
gs to explore. There are multiple chests i
y to stay higher up so you can snipe at enen
r below you. Once you have a weapon, try
scaffolding that goes across this area. As a
ild a ramp that takes you higher than your

## There Are Strange-Shaped Watchtowers around the Outskirts of the Island

Along the coastline of the island, you'll discover a small collection of massive wooden watchtowers that are shaped like different animals and objects. Consider landing on top of any of these towers and smashing your way down to discover chests and other useful weapons, ammo, and loot items. If you're approaching any of them on foot, you can always smash your way inside and climb upward using pre-created stairs or ramps you build yourself.

There's a llama-shaped tower at map coordinates B1.5, just outside of Junk Junction.

This area, located at map coordinates I9.5 isn't a tower, but it is where you'll find an RV surrounded by a bunch of junk. Open the chest if you find once here, and harvest everything in the area to collect resources. Here in the desert, smash open any random objects you encounter. You'll often find something useful inside.

This tall wooden tower, found between map coordinates I4.5 and J4.5, isn't shaped like an animal, but it's still work exploring in order to collect the items inside. Keep an eye on the storm's location, and make sure you'll have time to reach a safe part of the island once the storm expands and moves.

Located between map coordinates I2.5 and J2.5 is this house with a large wooden tower above it. There are chests and plenty of other useful weapons, ammo, and loot items to be found here. It's a nice, remote place to land and quickly build up your arsenal.

## How to Choose the Ideal Landing Location

One of the very first decisions you'll need to make at the start of each match is where on the island you want to land. First, while you're hanging out in the pre-deployment area, or when you first board the Battle Bus, check out the island map that shows the random route across the island that the bus will take.

When choosing a landing location, here are some things to consider:

- Do you want to land within one of the popular points of interest, knowing that you'll likely encounter enemy soldiers and need to fight almost immediately? If you choose this option, you'll need to find a weapon and be prepared to fight within seconds after landing.
- If you plan to land within one of the newly added points of interest, whether or not it's labeled on the island map, it's going to be a popular landing destination. Gamers always want to check out what's new. Thus, you'll definitely encounter enemy soldiers immediately upon landing.
- Out of the up to 99 other gamers participating in each match, many will jump from the Battle Bus at the very start of its journey across the island. Others will wait until the very last second before taking their leap off the bus. As a result, whatever points of interest are close to the start or end of the bus route will be popular during that match.
- Points of interest near the center of the island always tend to be popular. Many of the routes the Battle Bus could take go directly over this area, plus when you start a match near the center of the island, you typically don't have to travel as much to stay clear of the storm once it begins to expand.

A common strategy amongst expert *Fortnite: Battle Royale* players is to land in an unpopular spot where they'll likely find an abundance of weapons, ammo, and loot items right away. For example, the roof of the house located at the edge of the island, between map coordinates I2.5 and J2.5.

After quickly building up your arsenal, travel inward, avoiding the storm and any popular points of interest until you're close to the final circle and the End Game. Along the way, collect an abundance of resources (wood, stone, and metal), and be sure to search the buildings and structures you encounter.

By avoiding any points of interest early on, you dramatically decrease your chances of encountering enemy soldiers and being forced to fight. Instead, you can focus on building up the perfect arsenal for the End Game, while stocking up on supplies and resources. You won't earn as many experience points taking this approach, but you'll likely stay alive longer during each match.

# SECTION 5
## 15 TIPS FOR SAFELY EXPLORING THE ISLAND

The tips and strategies outlined in this section will help you survive longer and defeat more enemies as you explore the island. Be sure to check out "Section 9—Winning Battles and Matches" for additional tips on how to survive the final circle and End Game.

### Strategies That'll Help You Stay Alive Longer

**Tip #1**—As you explore each point of interest, always look and listen for chests. You'll also often discover weapons, ammo, ammo boxes, and loot items lying out in the open (on the ground). These items are sometimes hidden behind, above, or below objects. Here, weapons were found on the ground within the locker rooms at the soccer field found at coordinates C5 on the map.

**Tip #2**—There are many houses on the island. All look different from the outside, but on the inside, each contains several levels and multiple rooms. It's often within the attic, basement, or garage of these homes where you'll find chests. Within individual rooms, you'll sometimes discover weapons, ammo, and loot items lying on the ground.

**Tip #3**—Anytime you encounter an open door as you're about to enter a building or structure, this means that another soldier has already been there and could still be inside, so proceed with caution. If someone else has already explored that structure, chances are they've grabbed all of the useful items inside. One option is to hide outside, wait for the soldier to exit the structure and then ambush him. If you defeat that soldier, you can grab all of the items they've collected. To trick your opponents, consider closing doors behind you after entering or exiting a structure (or a room within a structure).

**Tip #4**—If you discover a cellar door outside of a home that leads to a basement, smash open the door with your pickaxe and explore that basement. You'll almost always discover a chest, as well as other items. If the cellar door has already been smashed, chances are someone has already explored the basement.

-There are several ways to enter a structure. You can lan d smash your way downward. You can enter through t 's also possible to smash through a wall to gain acces option is to build a ramp outside of the structure th oof. From the roof, smash your way down. If you're in ou know enemy soldiers are lurking, consider entering ough the backdoor, if applicable, in case they're hiding a ttack anyone who enters the front door.

-Before entering into a house or building, if there's a side. You can shoot at enemies through a window and r at least scout out what's inside to see if it's worth ent

-Always try to stay as high up as possible (above poten lost of the time, this gives you a huge tactical advantage er to shoot downward at an enemy with better accurac

eed to pass between two structures that are close to of exiting one, walking on the ground, and entering sider staying high up and building a bridge between

...tures. Anytime you're higher than your opponents, you'll be ...ntage during a fire fight.

...8—Anytime you're forced to travel out in the open on gr... ...always move quickly. Run in a zigzag (random) pattern and ... ...d down to make yourself a difficult target to hit. Be prepar... ...behind nearby objects or build defensive walls around you if s... ...starts shooting in your direction.

...9—If the need arises to walk through swamps or lakes, in Loot ...her areas, this can be a slow process. You'll be out in the oper... ...erable to attack. Consider building a bridge over the water to t... ...ss faster. Another alternative is to keep jumping as you attem... ...orward in the water.

...10—Whenever you're inside exploring a structure, the noises ...e will alert nearby enemies of your location. Walking, run... ...ing/closing doors, smashing objects, and building all make sou... ...duce the sound your soldier makes while moving around in...

**p #11**—When inside any building, house, or structure, don't forg__ __ou're able to gather resources by smashing walls, floors, ceilings, f__ __ture, appliances, and other objects. For example, smashing me__ __ppliances in a home will generate metal. Smashing wooden furnitu__ __r walls will generate wood, and smashing brick walls or fences will ge__ __rate stone.

**p #12**—Sometimes, to reach a hidden room or attic from within __ __ome or building, you'll need to smash through a wall, floor, or ceilin__ __ there's a chest behind a wall, listen for the sound chests make as y__ __et close. You'll hear the sound, even if you can't see the chest. In oth__ __tuations, you may need to build a platform or ramp inside of a stru__ __re in order to reach something worthwhile.

ytime you approach a cliff, do not jump off of the edge. You'll lik
re yourself when you reach the bottom. Instead, slide down the c
you'll land unharmed.

**#13**—As you prepare to enter into the End Game portion of a mat
ke sure you have one or two projectile explosive weapons on ha
ch as a rocket launcher), as well as a sniper rifle. You'll also w
east one weapon you can use for close- to mid-range combat, a
ity of ammo for all of your weapons.

**#14**—You never know when you'll get into an unexpected fight
injured during a match (from a fall or the storm, for example).
keep you alive longer, carry a Chug Jug (or at least a Med Kit a
ge Shield Potion) with you at all times, especially during the la
ges of a match.

nember, it takes time to consume or use a health and/or shi
enerating tool, so make sure you're in a safe location before us
of them. Check out "Section 7—Finding and Using Loot Items"
ails about other loot items that will boost your health and/or shie

# SECTION 6
## FINDING, COLLECTING, AND USING WEAPONS

**S**cattered throughout the island (particularly within points of interest) are hundreds of different types of weapons to collect, store in your backpack, and use against adversaries.

The weapon categories firearms and explosives typically fall into include:

- Assault Rifles
- Bolt Action Sniper Rifles
- Crossbows (These have been removed from the game, but could make a return in the future.)
- Explosive Weapons (including Grenade Launchers, Guided Missile Launchers, and Rocket Launchers)
- Grenades
- Hand Cannons
- Miniguns
- Pistols (and Suppressed Pistols)
- Pump-Action Shotguns
- Remote Explosives
- Revolvers
- Rifles
- Semi-Automatic Sniper Rifles
- Shotguns
- SMGs (Sub Machine Guns)
- Sniper Rifles
- Tactical Shotguns
- Tactical SMGs
- Thermal Scoped Assault Rifles

New weapons and weapon categories are added to the game almost weekly, while some previously introduced weapons get retired, or their capabilities are tweaked.

Many *Fortnite* gamers agree that the most useful weapon to master using is any type of shotgun. There are many types of shotguns to choose from. At close- to mid-range, they are more powerful than a pistol. When viewing the Backpack Inventory screen, details about the selected weapon/item you're holding are displayed. Here, details about a "rare" Pump Shotgun are displayed.

Shotguns can be used in close-range to mid-range combat situations, or even at a distance when no better-suited weapons are available. From a distance, shotguns are harder to aim accurately than a rifle with a scope, for example. When using a shotgun, always try for a headshot to inflict the most damage onto your target.

Each category of weapon can be used for a different purpose. Based on the type of enemy encounter you're experiencing at any given moment, it's essential you choose the most appropriate weapon at your disposal.

Before engaging in a firefight, consider:

- The types of weapons currently in your backpack and available to you.
- The amount of ammo you currently have for each weapon. Be sure to pick up as much ammo as you can throughout each match.
- The distance between you and your opponent.

- Your surroundings, and whether your weapon will need to destroy a barrier, fortress wall, or shielding before it can inflict damage on an enemy.
- Your own skill level as a gamer, and your speed when it comes to selecting, targeting/aiming, and firing your weapon.

powerful weapon with no ammo is useless. Collect ammo from chest upply Drops, Loot Llamas, Ammo Boxes (shown), and from defeate nemies. Ammo boxes are green. They do not glow or make a soun hey're often found on the ground, on shelves, or behind other objec uch as furniture or under staircases within a home or building). Loo mmo can also be found lying out in the open, on the ground, in mar reas of the island.

## Four Tips to Improve Your Shooting Accuracy

Regardless of which weapon you're using, your aim improves when you're crouching.

While it's often necessary to be running or jumping at the same time you're firing a weapon, your aiming accuracy improves when you're standing still.

You almost always have an advantage when you're higher up than your opponent and shooting in a downward direction.

Once a weapon is selected, tap on the Aim icon (on the right side of the screen) to zoom in and more precisely target your enemy. This offers far more precision than if you just pull the trigger on a weapon while you're facing an enemy. When you're aiming a weapon, you can stand still, crouch down (ideal), walk, run, or tiptoe, but when moving, you'll travel slower.

## Understand How Weapons Are Rated and Categorized

While every weapon can cause damage and ultimately defeat your adversaries (with one or more direct hits), each is rated based on several criteria, including its rarity. Weapons are color-coded with a hue around them to showcase their rarity.

Weapons with a **whiteish/gray** hue are "Common."

Weapons with a **green** hue are "Uncommon."

Weapons with a **blue** hue are "Rare."

Weapons with a **purple** hue are "Epic."

egendary" weapons with a **yellowish/orange** hue are hard to fin xtra powerful, and very rare. If you're able to obtain one, grab it!

is possible to collect several of the same weapon, but each could hav different rarity. So, if you collect two of the same weapon, and one re but the second is legendary, definitely keep the legendary weapo nd trade the other for something else when you find a replacement.

ne rarity of a weapon contributes heavily to its Damage Per Secon PS) Rating. The DPS Rating for a legendary weapon is much highe aan the DPS Rating for an identical weapon that has a common rarit r example.

- **DPS Rating**—Use this rating to help estimate a weapon's power. It does not take into account things like accuracy of your aim, or the extra damage you can inflict by making a headshot, for example. In general, DPS is calculated by multiplying the damage the weapon can cause by its fire rate.

- **Damage Rating**—This is a numeric rating based on how much potential damage a weapon can cause per direct hit.
- **Fire Rate**—This refers to the number of bullets fired per second. Some of the most powerful weapons have a slow Fire Rate, so to inflict the most damage, your aim needs to be perfect. Otherwise, during the time in-between shots, your enemy could move, or launch their own counter attack.
- **MAG (Magazine) Capacity**—This is the total number of ammunition rounds (or bullets) the weapon can hold at once before it needs to be reloaded. Reloading a weapon takes valuable time, during which your soldier will be vulnerable to attack. Your enemy could also move, meaning you'll need to re-aim your weapon.
- **Reload Time**—This is the number of seconds it takes to reload the weapon, assuming you have replacement ammo available. Some of the most powerful weapons have a very slow reload time, so if your shooting accuracy isn't great, you'll be at a disadvantage.

There are plenty of websites, including: IGN.com (www.ign.com/wikis/fortnite/Weapons), Gameskinny.com (www.gameskinny.com/9mt22/complete-fortnite-battle-royale-weapons-stats-list), and RankedBoost.com (https://rankedboost.com/fortnite/best-weapons-tier-list), that provide the current stats for each weapon offered in *Fortnite*, based on the latest tweaks made to the game. Just make sure when you look at this information online, it refers to the most recently released version of *Fortnite: Battle Royale*.

## Choose Your Arsenal Wisely

Based on where you are, what challenges you're currently encountering, and what you anticipate your needs will be, stock your backpack with the weapons and tools you believe you'll need. For example, as you prepare for the final fights at the end of a match, a sniper rifle as well as a grenade launcher, rocket launcher, or guided missile launcher are essential. You'll likely be hiding in your fortress and trying to defeat the final enemies who are hiding (at a distance) in their own fortresses. The weapons you use must be able to destroy fortress walls and inflict damage on your enemies.

If during the final minutes of a match an enemy rushes you (or uses a Launch Pad to quickly approach), be prepared to engage in close- or mid-range combat. Having a Chug Jug (or other HP and shield power-up essentials) on hand could keep you alive if you're harmed in battle.

## Know What Your Backpack Can Hold

Your soldier's backpack has six main slots and can hold six items, including the pickaxe. That leaves five slots for carrying different types of guns, alternative weapons (such as a trap, remote explosive, or grenades), and/or loot items (such as med kits, chug jugs, shield potions, or bandages). Make smart inventory decisions throughout each match.

The Backpack Inventory screen allows you to view what you have and organize the backpack's contents. As a match progresses, your arsenal and health/shield recovery needs will change, so plan accordingly.

To make accessing content from your backpack faster during battles, you're able to reorganize what's inside from the Backpack Inventory screen.

When viewing the Backpack Inventory screen, highlight an item on the right side of the screen to see a description or details about it on the left side. If you highlight a weapon in your inventory (a "legendary" minigun is shown here), you'll see details about that weapon. If you select a type of ammo, you'll discover what weapon(s) that ammo can be used with, and how much of it you currently have on hand.

# SECTION 7

## FINDING AND USING LOOT ITEMS

Just as powerful weapons and ammo can be found throughout the island, a selection of loot items is also available. Loot can help boost your HP, increase your shields, or provide additional weapons or tools that will help you stay alive. Epic Games continuously adds new types of loot to the game.

### Keep Your Soldier Healthy

Displayed continuously in the top-left corner of the screen is your soldier's Health and Shield meter. Both can go from zero to 100. The health meter (displayed in green) starts at 100. Each time a solder receives damage, their health meter decreases. When it reaches zero, a soldier is immediately eliminated from the match.

At the start of a match, a soldier's Shield meter (displayed in blue) is at zero. To activate and increase shields, a shield power-up item, such as a shield potion, mushroom, or Chug Jug must be consumed or used. Once shields are active, if a soldier receives damage from a weapon attack, their shields get depleted first. Then, once the Shield meter reaches zero, the soldier's Health meter starts to be impacted by damage that gets inflicted. Keep in mind, shields do not protect against falls.

Regardless of which power-up items you use to replenish your health or shields during a match, neither meter can go above 100.

## How to Acquire Loot Items

here are a variety of ways to acquire and collect loot items during
atch, including:

- They can be found lying out in the open, on the ground.
- After defeating an enemy, you can grab whatever loot items
  that were previously in their possession. This is one of the
  biggest perks to defeating enemies in battle.
- They can be purchased from Vending Machines (using
  wood, stone, or metal as in-game currency).
- They're sometimes included within chests.
- They're sometimes included within Loot Llamas.
- They're sometimes found within Supply Drops.

uring matches, Supply Drops (which looks like a balloon carrying
ue box) will fall from the sky. This is a rare occurrence. When yc
oproach and open a Supply Drop, you'll receive a random collection

when you open a Supply Drop, you'll receive at leas
eapon (with a yellowish/orange hue), as well as a st
ne, and/or metal, along with other items.

than Supply Drops are Loot Llamas. These look lik
the shape of a llama. When you smash one open
with a random collection of weapons, ammo, loot i

Scattered randomly throughout the island (typically within points of interest) are Vending Machines. Each offers a small, random collection of weapons and loot items that can be purchased using wood, stone, or metal.

Be sure to approach Supply Drops, Loot Llamas, and Vending Machines with extreme caution. Instead of collecting what's inside, some gamers choose to boobytrap them with remote explosives, or hide at a distance (with their sniper rifle in hand), and then ambush anyone who approaches. You too can use this as an easy strategy for defeating enemies.

If you make it safely to a Supply Drop, Loot Llama, or Vending Machine, consider building walls around it and yourself, so you can safely open it, and then grab and organize the contents without the fear of being attacked.

## Loot Items and How to Use Them

s of June 2018, the following is a list of loot items you'll likely encou
r on the island. Some items are considered rare and much harder
nd than others.

pples—You'll occasionally find apples lying on the ground under tree
/hen you pick up and consume an apple, your Health meter gains
oints (up to 100). However, you must consume an apple when ar
here you find it. You're not able to pick them up and store them
our backpack for later use.

**Bandages**—Each time a bandage is used, it replenishes 15 HP. A player can carry up to five bandages within their backpack in a single slot. It takes several seconds to use bandages, during which time a soldier is vulnerable to attack, so be sure you're well-hidden or protected when using this item.

**Boogie Bombs**—Toss one of these bombs at an opponent and they'll be forced to dance for five seconds while taking damage.

**Bouncer Trap**—When an enemy accidently steps on or activates this type of trap, he'll go flying into the air and land with a splat. These traps can be placed on floors or walls.

**Bush**—A bush can be worn by a soldier and used as camouflage. Be sure to crouch to avoid being seen. If there are other bushes in the area you'll blend right in. However, a bush offers no protection from attacks. If you start moving while camouflaged by a bush, an adversary will definitely notice and attack. This item is best used outside when standing still to avoid being detected by nearby enemies.

**ires**—Once activated, any soldier that stands
two HP per second, for up to 25 seconds (up to
that a soldier is vulnerable to attack during
campfire after building a protective barrier a
campfire or find a secure and secluded place
g with teammates, multiple people can take a
e's healing powers.

This item takes 15 seconds to drink, during v
nerable to attack unless he/she's protected. C
tores a soldier's HP *and* shield meter to 100 pe
e as you enter the later stages of a match, w
re difficult.

**lingers**—These explosive items look like a toilet plunger. Throw the : any object or enemy, and it'll attach. Within a few seconds, BOON nce a clinger is tossed and attaches to something, it'll turn blue whe ctivated. Within a few seconds, it generates an explosion that'll destro ything in the vicinity, plus damage (or defeat) enemies.

**renades**—Toss a grenade at an enemy, and it'll explode on impac irect hits cause the most damage, but even if the grenade lands clos an enemy, damage is still inflicted. Like most weapons (particular xplosives), grenades can also destroy structures or buildings.

**npulse Grenades**—This type of grenade inflicts damage to enemi nd throws them into the air, away from the point of impact.

**op Rocks**—Any time you explore a crater (at least during Season nances are you'll find Hop Rocks. Consume one or more of these rock nd for a short time, you will be able to jump higher and leap farthe ou'll also be protected from harm if you fall.

**Jetpacks**—When you find a jetpack, strap it onto your back when you need it, and you can fly through the air and navigate where you fly for a short time. Jetpacks were introduced as a temporarily item in *Fortnite: Battle Royale* and have since been removed from the game (also known as "vaulted"). Epic Games has reported, however, that it plans to bring them back occasionally, because they proved to be very popular.

**Launch Pad**—Activate this item to catapult your soldier into the air, and automatically utilize their glider. You can then guide your soldier around in mid-air for a few seconds. Use this tool, for example, to escape after being engulfed by the storm, or to flee from an attack. It allows you to move great distances quickly. While you're flying, you can still be shot at by enemies.

ate a Launch Pad, it must be placed on a flat surface. Er
mode and create one floor piece, and then place the
top of it.

to the Launch Pad and soar into the air. The glider will au
tivate. Steer your soldier around while in mid-air. You ca
ame Launch Pad and jump as many times as you want, b
up, it can't be moved.

**hield Potions**—Consuming this item increases your
by 25, but it takes several seconds to drink, during whi
dier is vulnerable to attack.

**s**—Restore your health to 100 percent each time a Me
takes 10 seconds to use a Med Kit, during which time yo
lnerable to attack.

**...ushrooms**—Found on the ground in swampy areas, when you pi... ...o and consumer a blue mushroom, your shields gain five points (u... ...o 100). You must consume a mushroom when and where you find... ...ou're not able to pick them up and store them in your backpack fo... ...ter use.

**...ort-a-Fort**—This insta-fort is made of metal, and instantly gets bui... ...hen you activate it. Use it for protection without having to manual... ...o any building. It requires no resources. Included within the Port-... ...ort are tires, allowing you to jump to the top of the fort (from th... ...side) with ease. In addition to offering protection, the top of a fo... ...rovides an ideal vantage point for shooting enemies in any directio...

...ny time you find tires on the island, jump c...
...up higher than you can jump yourself.

...osives—A soldier can carry up to 10 of the...
...ate it by attaching it to an object, wall, or...
...detonate it remotely from any distance av...
...ote explosive, lure your adversary to its lo...
...Just make sure you're far enough away...
...rself.

...s—Each time you drink a shield potion, you...
...50 (up to a maximum of 100). Drink two in...
...eplenish your soldier's shields. This item take...
...me, during which time your soldier is vulnera...

**Shopping Carts**—This is a relatively new way to move around the island, instead of walking or running. Shopping carts are placed randomly around the island and are rare.

If you find a shopping cart, push it up a hill, point it down the hill, give it a running start, and quickly jump in for a wild and fast ride. You'll cover a lot of distance fast. Epic Games has removed and then reintroduced shopping carts into the game multiple times, so they may or may not be available when you play.

**Slurp Juice**—As you drink this item, your HP and shield strength increases by one point every second (for up to 25 seconds). While you're drinking, your soldier must be standing still and is vulnerable to attack.

**Stink Bombs**—When tossed, these bombs generate an awful smell which will make your enemies run for cover (and receive damage at the same time). For every half-second an enemy is stuck in the stink cloud generated by the bomb, his health or shields drops by five points. The stink cloud lasts for nine seconds total.

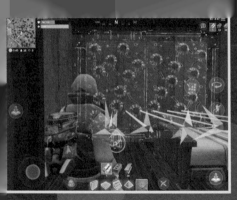

**Traps**—Set a trap on any structure's floor, wall, or ceiling and then leave it. When an opponent accidently activates the hidden trap, they'll receive mega-damage. Just make sure you don't set off the trap yourself once you've activated it, or you'll be the one getting hurt! Shown here is a trap being set up and activated on a wall within a cabin (located in Lonely Lodge).

This is what a trap looks like once it's been placed on a wall and activated. Typically, you'd place them where an enemy wouldn't see them. Traps can now be placed on ramps too. When you build a ramp, place a trap near the bottom to keep an enemy from following you.

A trap waiting to be picked up by the soldier is shown here. It can be added to her backpack for later use.

**l Terrain Karts (ATKs)** — ATKs provide a fast and extremely fun way t around the island. Practice performing stunts while you're drivin en if your ATK goes airborne, you will not be injured as a result of th l. While these vehicles are tough, they're not indestructible. They ca destroyed by enemy attacks, for example.

roughout the island, but mainly in the desert area surrounding Paradi lms, you may discover Rifts at random locations. Step into it and your so er will be catapulted into the air. His or her glider will activate when it's tin land. Use a Rift to travel a good distance quickly or to escape an atta om enemies. Stepping into a Rift can also help you outrun the storm.

# SECTION 8

## RESOURCE GATHERING AND BUILDING

Throughout every match, gathering or harvesting resources (wood, stone, and metal) is a key component of the game. Once collected, resources are used to purchase items from Vending Machines, and to build structures, such as ramps and fortresses.

### How to Collect Wood, Stone, and Metal

There are several ways to collect or harvest resources. These include:

- Defeating enemies and collecting the resources they gathered.
- Finding and grabbing wood, stone, or metal icons scattered randomly throughout the island. Each provides a bundle of a specific resources. These resource icons are also found within chests, supply drops, and loot llamas.
- Using the pickaxe, smash trees or any wooden items (including structures) to collect wood. Harvesting the largest trees, with the thickest trunks, generates much more wood than smaller trees. Smashing wooden pallets is also a great source of wood.
- Using the pickaxe, smash stone piles, or anything made of brick, for example, to collect stone.
- Using the pickaxe, smash vehicles, cargo containers, or any metal objects found on the island (including kitchen appliances or machinery) to collect metal.

e pickaxe to smash trees allows you to gather wood. Th
Wailing Woods tend to be among the largest found

g any type of vehicle or metal object with the picka
ou to collect metal.

Use the pickaxe to smash any structure, such as the wall, floor, or ceiling of a home or building—this allows you to collect whatever material that you're smashing is made from. A wooden house, for example, generates wood, while a brick house (or chimney) generates stone. If you attempt to shoot at or blow up a structure (as opposed to smashing at it with the pickaxe), this does not allow you to collect resources.

## Basic Building Techniques You'll Need to Master

Building is an important component of *Fortnite: Battle Royale*, and it's a skill you'll need to practice in order to master it. When it comes to building, speed is essential.

Upon entering into Building mode, you need to know exactly what icons to tap in order to quickly build the type of structure you need, when you need it, sometimes while you're being attacked by enemies. To practice building, consider traveling to a remote and deserted portion of the island where you won't be disturbed. Collect a bunch of resources, and then practice quickly building ramps, basic defensive structures (such as a 1x1 fortress), and more elaborate fortresses.

After entering into Building mode, choose which resource (wood, stone, or metal) you want to build with, based on what you've collected and have on hand. Tap on the icon for the resource you want to use. Wood is the fastest material to build with, but it offers the least amount of protection. Use it to construct ramps or basic defensive structures. Building with stone takes a bit longer, but it can withstand stronger attacks and keep you protected a bit longer.

Metal is the strongest, but slowest material to build with.

If you need to collect items from a defeated enemy, make a purchase from a Vending Machine, or require protection when using a health or shield power-up that takes several seconds to consume or use, quickly build four walls around yourself using the strongest material you have available.

To protect yourself quickly when you're being attacked, consider building a vertical wall in front of you, and directly behind it, build a ramp. Then crouch down behind the ramp. An enemy will need to destroy both building pieces before your soldier gets harmed.

Add sides to this basic protective structure so it offers more protection from more angles, in case you get flanked from the sides too.

To reach an area higher up, build a basic ramp. Keep in mind, if an enemy destroys the bottom of the ramp while you're on it, you'll come crashing to the ground and could get injured or even defeated by the damage (depending on how far you fall). Ramps can be built almost anywhere outside or even inside homes, buildings, or structures to help you reach something higher up. This ramp leads to the roof of the lodge building in Lonely Lodge.

ramp building strategy is to create doub
resources, but it allows you to move b
u're being attacked, you can leap to the
crumble. This approach also makes it h
your exact location. Ramps allow you to
er up than your opponent gives you a tac
g an attack.

ces, height is more important than securit
upward, and then shoot down at enemie
both sides of the ramp for added prote
es not have time to shoot and destroy yo
p of it, you'll be at an advantage. It's safe f
ree stories when leaping out of a self-ma
m any higher, injury (or worse) will result.

## Learn to Quickly Build "1x1" Fortresses

A 1x1 fortress is simply four walls around you, with a ramp in the center, that goes up multiple levels. Using wood allows you to build with the greatest speed, but using metal offers the greatest protection. Keep practicing until you're able to build this type of fortress very quickly, without having to think too much about it.

Here's how to build a 1x1 fortress:

First build four vertical walls so they surround you. If you're not on a flat surface, start by building one floor panel on the ground.

In the center, build a ramp. As the ramp is being constructed, jump on it.

repeating this process to add as many levels to your fort a[s]
making it taller.

[ea]sily enter and exit, go into Edit mode and build a door o[r]
[2n]d level.

onsider adding four pyramid-shaped roo
added protection when you peek out. F
on from directly above as well, add a flat
oof piece directly over your head. This 1x1

the same structures can be built using sto
ion of wood, stone, and metal. From the
you turn on the Auto Material Change op
ches between wood, stone, and/or meta
esource as you're building. This speeds u
ng on the Turbo Building feature also spe
quickly using the same type of building tile
on for example)

## A Tall and Sturdy Fortress Is Often Necessary During the End Game

During the End Game, when you're in the final circle and competing against the most skilled gamers who also managed to survive this long, establishing a strong and sturdy base is often essential. Remember, height is important. If you build a wider base, enemies won't be able to easily tell where within the base you're hiding in between your attacks (using your projectile weapons or rifle with a scope).

The best way to learn building techniques for End Game fortresses is to stay in Spectator Mode after you get eliminated from matches and watch more experienced gamers play. You should also watch the online streams from *Fortnite: Battle Royale* experts on YouTube or Twitch.tv.

# SECTION 9
## WINNING BATTLES AND MATCHES

Those final minutes of a match (known as the "End Game")—when the circle becomes very small, and only a few of the most highly skilled enemy soldiers remain alive—are when you'll need to step up and showcase your survival, building, and fighting skills—often at the same time—in order to win the match and become the last person standing.

Step one is to be prepared. Go into the final circle with your HP and Shield meters fully charged. Plus, have plenty of resources on hand (at least 1,500 to 2,000 wood, stone, and/or metal is ideal). It's also necessary to have the right assortment of weapons in your arsenal. A grenade launcher and/or rocket launcher, as well as a sniper rifle (or rifle with a scope) are definitely must-have weapons.

### 12 End Game Strategies to Help You Prepare to Win Any Match

Preparation is the key when you enter into the End Game in hopes of winning a match. It's also important to stay calm, watch what your enemies are doing, and stay focused on your objectives.

Here are 12 End Game strategies to help you win:

1. Choose the best location to build your fortress, from which you'll make your final stand in battle. If you're in a good position, you can be more aggressive with your attacks. However, if you're in the dead-center of the final circle, you will become the center of attention, which probably isn't good.
2. Make sure your fortress is tall, well-fortified, and that it offers an excellent, 360-degree view of the surrounding area from the top level.

3. If your fortress gets destroyed, be prepared to move quick, and have a backup strategy in place that will help to ensure your survival. Having the element of surprise for your attacks gives you a tactical advantage. Don't become an easy target to hit. Keep moving around your fort, or while you're out in the open!

4. During the End Game, don't engage every remaining player. Allow them to fight amongst themselves to reduce their numbers, plus reduce or even deplete their ammo and resources.

5. Only rely on a sniper rifle (or scoped rifle) to make long-range shots if you have really good aim. Otherwise use explosive weapons that'll cause damage over a wide area, such as a Grenade Launcher or Rocket Launcher.

6. Always keep tabs on the location of your remaining enemies during the End Game. Don't allow them to sneak up behind you, for example. Even if your back is to the storm, an enemy could enter the storm temporarily, and then emerge behind you to launch a surprise attack if you lose track of their location. Gamers that use the storm to their tactical advantage are referred to as "storm riders." If you lose track of an enemy who you know is nearby, listen carefully for their movement.

7. Don't invest a lot of resources into a massive and highly fortified fortress until you know you're in the final circle during a match. Refer to the map and the displayed timer. Otherwise, when the storm expands and moves, you could find it necessary to abandon your fort, and then need to build another one quickly, in a not-so-ideal location. Having to rebuild will use up your resources.

8. Base pushers are enemies that aren't afraid to leave their fortress and attempt to attack yours during the final minutes of a match. Be prepared to deal with their close-range threat.

9. If two or three enemies remain, focus on one at a time. Determine who appears to be the most imminent and largest threat. Be prepared to change priorities at a moment's notice, based on the actions of your enemies.

10. Some final battles take place on ramps, not from within fortresses. In this situation, speed/quick reflexes, getting higher up than your enemy, and good aim with the proper weapon are the keys to winning. Try to destroy the bottom of an enemy's ramp to make the whole thing come crashing down. The soldier standing on the ramp will be injured or defeated, based on how far he or she falls to the ground.

11. Have a Chug Jug on hand to replenish your HP and shields if you're attacked, and incur damage, but are not defeated. Make sure you're well protected when you drink the Chug Jug. Med Kits are also great for maintaining HP during End Games.

12. Study the live streams created by expert *Fortnite* players (on YouTube and Twitch.tv) to learn their End Game strategies and see how they react to various challenges.

# FORTNITE: BATTLE ROYALE RESOURCES

Pro gamers around the world have created YouTube channels, online forums, and blogs focused exclusively on *Fortnite: Battle Royale*. You can also watch pro players compete online and describe their best strategies or check out the coverage of *Fortnite: Battle Royale* published by leading gaming websites and magazines.

On YouTube (www.youtube.com) or Twitch.TV (www.twitch.tv/directory/game/Fortnite), in the Search field, enter the search phrase "Fortnite: Battle Royale" to discover many game-related channels, livestreams, and pre-recorded videos.

Be sure to check out these awesome online resources that will help you become a better *Fortnite: Battle Royale* player:

| WEBSITE OR YOUTUBE CHANNEL NAME | DESCRIPTION | URL |
|---|---|---|
| Fandom's *Fortnite* Wiki | Discover the latest news and strategies related to *Fortnite*. | http://fortnite.wikia.com/wiki/Fortnite_Wiki |
| FantasticalGamer | A popular YouTuber who publishes *Fortnite* tutorial videos. | www.youtube.com/user/FantasticalGamer |
| FBR Insider | The *Fortnite: Battle Royale* Insider website offers game-related news, tips, and strategy videos. | www.fortniteinsider.com |
| *Fortnite* Scout | Check your personal player stats, and analyze your performance using a bunch of colorful graphs and charts. Also check out the stats of other *Fortnite* players. | www.fortnitescout.com |

| | | |
|---|---|---|
| *Fortnite* Stats & Leaderboard | This is an independent website that allows you to view your own *Fortnite*-related stats, or discover the stats from the best players in the world. | https://fortnitestats.com |
| *Game Informer* Magazine's *Fortnite* Coverage | Discover articles, reviews, and news about *Fortnite* published by *Game Informer* magazine. | www.gameinformer.com/ search/searchresults. aspx?q=Fortnite |
| *Game Skinny* Online Guides | A collection of topic-specific strategy guides related to *Fortnite*. | www.gameskinny.com/tag/ fortnite-guides/ |
| GameSpot's *Fortnite* Coverage | Check out the news, reviews, and game coverage related to *Fortnite: Battle Royale* that's been published by GameSpot. | www.gamespot.com/fortnite |
| IGN Entertainment's *Fortnite* Coverage | Check out all IGN's past and current coverage of *Fortnite*. | www.ign.com/wikis/fortnite |
| Jason R. Rich's Website and Social Media Feeds | Share your *Fortnite* gameplay strategies with this book's author and learn about his other books. | www.JasonRich.com www.FortniteGameBooks.com Twitter: @JasonRich7 Instagram: @JasonRich7 |
| Microsoft's Xbox One *Fortnite* Website | Learn about and acquire *Fortnite: Battle Royale* if you're an Xbox One gamer. | www.microsoft.com/en-US/ store/p/Fortnite-Battle-Royalee/ BT5P2X999VH2 |
| MonsterDface YouTube and Twitch.tv Channels | Watch video tutorials and live game streams from an expert *Fortnite* player. | www.youtube.com/user/ MonsterdfaceLive www.Twitch.tv/MonsterDface |
| Ninja | Check out the live and recorded game streams from Ninja, one of the most highly skilled *Fortnite: Battle Royale* players in the world on Twitch. tv and YouTube. | www.twitch.tv/ ninja_fortnite_hyper www.youtube.com/user/ NinjasHyper |
| Nomxs | A YouTube and Twitch.tv channel hosted by online personality Simon Britton (Nomxs). He too is one of *Fortnite*'s top-ranked players. | https://youtu.be/np-8cmsUZmc or www.twitch.tv/ videos/259245155 |

| | | |
|---|---|---|
| Official Epic Games YouTube Channel for *Fortnite* | The official *Fortnite* YouTube channel. | www.youtube.com/user/epicfortnite |
| Official Facebook page for *Fortnite* from Epic Games | This is the official Facebook page from Epic Games that covers all things related *to Fortnite: Battle Royale* | www.facebook.com/FortniteGame |
| Official *Fortnite* Website from Epic Games | Learn all about *Fortnite: Battle Royale*, as well as the paid editions of *Fortnite*. | www.Fortnite.com |
| Official Twitter feed for *Fortnite* from Epic Games | The official *Fortnite* Twitter feed. | https://twitter.com/fortnitegame (@fortnitegame) |
| Sony's PS4 *Fortnite* Website | Learn about and acquire *Fortnite* if you're a PS4 gamer. | www.playstation.com/en-us/games/fortnite-ps4 |
| Turtle Beach Corp. | This is one of several companies that make awesome quality gaming headsets that work any mobile device that has a 3.5mm headphone jack. Being able to hear crystal-clear sound and hold conversations with fellow gamers is essential when playing *Fortnite*. | www.turtlebeach.com |

## Your Adventure Continues . . .

Just when you think you've mastered *Fortnite: Battle Royale*'s Solo gameplay mode and you're able to occasionally win matches, Epic Games releases updates that require gamers to master new skills, explore new areas of the island, and utilize new items and weapons in order to achieve victory. At the same time, as other gamers become more experienced playing *Fortnite: Battle Royale*, it makes them increasingly more difficult to defeat.

And then there are the other *Fortnite: Battle Royale* gameplay modes, like Duos and Squads, along with the other team-oriented gameplay modes that Epic Games introduces for short periods of time. When you experience the game with one or more teammates, or play a 50 vs 50 match (as opposed to a 1 vs 99 Solo match), the overall gameplay experience during each match is vastly different, yet equally exciting and challenging.

Thanks to the *Fortnite: Battle Royale* for iOS and Android versions, gamers can experience their favorite game virtually anytime and anywhere their smartphone or tablet has a continuous internet connection. Just like the versions of the game for the PC, Mac, Xbox One, Playstation 4, and Nintendo Switch, the mobile version continues to evolve with each new game update released by Epic Games.

To become a true *Fortnite: Battle Royale* champion, keep practicing and work on mastering the tips and strategies outlined in this guide, while constantly trying to improve your building speed, weapon aiming accuracy, survival tactics, and overall gaming skills.

Stay focused! Keep practicing! But most important of all, have fun!

Jason R. Rich, the author of the guide you're currently reading, has teamed up with Sky Pony Press (an imprint of Skyhorse Publishing), to write an entire series of unofficial, full-color *Fortnite: Battle Royale* strategy guides (each sold separately).

To get your hands on these information-packed strategy guides, visit your favorite bookstore, or when visiting Amazon.com or BN.com, within the Search field, type, "*Fortnite, Jason R. Rich*" to find and order the latest guides. You can also visit www.FortniteGameBooks.com for more information.